SUBCONSCIOUS SKILLS SUCCESS

10 Simple Strategies
You Should Know

Jonathan Chase

Published in Great Britain in 2019
Under the Bow Books label by
SubSkills Training Ltd.

Enquiries should be addressed to
team@subskillstraining.com

First printed edition 2019
British Library Cataloguing in Publication Data
ISBN Number: 978-1-9165026-3-5

Dedication

For all the mind owners that have allowed me to
help them play and imagine...
You've taught me everything.

Contents

Introduction

EVERYTHING BEGINS AND ENDS IN YOUR MIND

Your Subconscious process is where all of your responses happen, all of your decisions are made or directed by it. Emotive, playful, imaginative, creative and experimental. It has the maturity of a bright 9 – 10 year old. You can't master, direct or reprogram it, your intellectual conscious can learn to live with it and guide it. When you do, miracles can happen.

The aim of this book is simply to show you how to get the best and fastest response from your subconscious process as and when you need it.

Jonathan Chase used his SubSkills to get from his coal mining background to award winning Edutainer hypnotist and the Stage of Las Vegas, despite Muscular Dystrophy and using a wheelchair.

Now he teaches you fast and fun strategies from his 4 decades of experience to claim the Subconscious Skills Success you want!

Nothing gets you to success faster than focus and clarity on the little things you do to get what you want.

"Jonathan's fantasmagorical and eclectic style has drawn me in, educated me and sent me out with more confidence and expertise. Jonathan has so much to offer, whether it's a book publication, or business training, mentalism (my favourite part), or tales of his varied and illustrious career. It's all completely absorbing. If you haven't trained, worked with or consulted Jonathan yet, you should!."
Kate Guest -*Trainer Speaker*

The strategies in here work, some have more longevity than others but you can use them to guide your subconscious immediately.

They are fast, fun and effective. Take the first steps to work with your subconscious so you have less stress in your life's enterprise.

Please give us feedback on how they work for you.

https://SubSkillsTraining.com

What Is Subconscious Skills Success?

Jane: So Jon, in a short sentence or two, what is Subconscious Skills Success ?

Jon: SubSkills are the little things you do to get what you want, and it doesn't matter if you're professionally or personally communicating, when you get Subconscious skills success you'll get Comfortable Confidence, Increased Influence and Personal Presence.

SubSkills are skills that make up part of a larger skill. For instance adding, subtracting, multiplying are sub-skills of numeracy. Reading and writing are sub-skills of literacy.

Skills of course are the ability to do something well, in this particular case what we need to do well is communicate by simply being us, using the exact same skills that have got you here all the way from infancy, and using them deliberately.

I've spent a few decades experimenting with and developing my subconscious methods from actual practice in mentalism, mesmerism, metaphysics, mentoring, anchoring, NLP, stage and speaking performance, and, helping private clients, from business and the professions, become more effective and engaging in presentation, negotiation and communicating better in all their relationships...

If you are a business owner or professional; sell, tell, teach, train, coach, consult, write, present, speak, lead, have a good sense of humour, are open to a very direct, practical and experiential approach of what some call coaching (I take few prisoners) and want to be more successful, then I know what's in this book and the follow on classes, will help you.

Success and Onions

Jane: Okay so when we are mentoring we start
         with what we call a Foundation Focus
         interview and the first question is always
         what does success mean to you? So
         Jonathan Chase… Success?

Jon: Well you know all success is subjective.
         And that means that most success is
         subconscious anyway because it's all
         about emotions.

         It's always about how you feel at the end
         of the day. Of course we have
         competitions in sports so we can see the
         winners as successful. And we can agree
         that people who get gongs and medals
         and awards are successful.

         Mostly people with loads of things and a
         high income are called a success and of

course they are, but then so is anybody who achieves their intent and what they set out to do.

And our success stories are often not what people expect, and we usually have many, many more than just one.

My favourite success story for me doesn't mean much to most people except maybe other stage hypnotists, but I'll tell it anyway.

Do you know why you cry when you chop onions?

An onion when it's cut into, releases an irritant known as syn-propanethial-S-oxide.

It stimulates the eyes lachrymal glands so they release tears.

Really strong onions also leave a burning sensation on your tongue and make your nose run as the smell activates your mucus defence system.

This reaction varies in people of course, but out of 10 people at least 8 are going to react instantly and the other couple will get there eventually.

What's this got to do with understanding the power of the subconscious imagination?

The question I always start coaching and classes with is a simple one, how will you know you're successful?

What will it look like when you hit that point in time, when you get that result, that reward that says yes, I'm successful?

For me, one of those times happened once upon a time ago…

There was one incident when I met, really met people's subconscious minds for the first time, and it was that exact same moment I knew I was successful being a hypnotist, specifically being a Stage Hypnotist.

And it was also the time when I understood the power of the subconscious mind.

Come back with me to a Midlands Coal Miner's sports and social working men's club back in their heyday of the late 80's.

Imagine a small stage, a few feet high, and wide enough to put around twelve chairs side by side.

At the back of the stage is a sequinned spangly curtain and stretching away into the room are four or five rows of tables with chairs either side.

On the tables are used bingo tickets and half drunk drinks, beer for the gentlemen and cherryB or cider for the ladies.

Every chair has an occupant, in this club, that's a couple of hundred people, some of them went up to thousands, but this is a small one, and at the back of the room there's children running around, eating crisps and drinking Vimto.

The bar is at the side and people are buying beers, the tills are tinging, and without doubt there's someone feeding a one armed bandit with last weeks wages.

Every Saturday these people are here, this is **their** place, **their** club. They're not here to see me in particular, they are here to play housey-housey (bingo), drink a few pints, well often *lots* of pints. To meet their mates socially and natter.

When you walk out on stage after being introduced badly by someone who's got you mixed up with last weeks act, you hit a wall of folded arms and a general atmosphere of;

"I've been in a hole in the ground for 7 and half hours a day, five days this week... go on... entertain me!"

Anyone who tells you it was easy to persuade those men and women to come on stage and entertain their friends by having their imaginations boosted... well it was a hard sell let me tell you.

But actually for me it was easy, because that is one of my subconscious skills. I'm very good at getting people to do stuff subconsciously. (Laughs) so is everyone else of course but the successful know they are.

This was my third paid show. The first one I'd died, that's showbiz for not done very well, the second had been much better but lacked a real gobsmacking showstopper.

So, this one, only my third show, I'd decided on presenting a routine that only a handful of hypnotists have been brave enough to do.

I first saw this routine in 1976 at Glasgow Empire performed by the first really modern stage hypnotist called Robert Halpern, and it was then that my love of theatre had come round to exciting my fascination in people's minds. And why people do stuff.

Halpern stuck people's hands together.

He invited them on stage, he freed their imaginations and allowed them to act like children and gave them the script of the story they were acting out; then towards the end of his show he gave them an onion and told them it was an apple.

Stage hypnotists often use imagining eating a lemon to get people's mouths to water, and we usually change or create smells that we know they'll react to. But apart from plain water it's very brave indeed to give people stuff to actually put in their mouths.

I don't know any American colleagues doing it, but they live in the land of 'Sue Theassoffyou' so perhaps it's safer to avoid such things....

You know it's very, very difficult to cut into an onion and not be forced to cry. To bite into an onion it's almost impossible.

On this particular evening I had 12 people in front of me and I'd got with me the strongest, smelliest Spanish onions Sainsbury's could supply. Naturally we'd peeled them in the dressing room and even just removing the inedible outer casing had my assistant having to re-do her mascara and blush.

I'd taken the precaution of asking the people who were with the people on stage if any of them had allergies or stomach problems like ulcers, allergies weren't around then, and had given the guy I thought was my best hypnotee, the suggestion that he was hungry and that he loved fruit.

I then, woke him and gave him an onion whilst reminding him it was beautifully tasting fruit.

He looked at it, smelt it, and bit into it…

Amazingly, he smiled, took another bite and crunched away a very happy man.

That boosted my confidence in my hypnotic skills and five minutes later all of them were eating the onions as if it were fruit with Gusto.

It was terrible.

I couldn't see. I was crying so hard because the stench of onion was strong. People in the third and fourth rows back from this stage were crying.

My friends on stage were arguing that they got the fruit and the others were eating an onion.

But.

Not one of them was reacting to onion. No tears, no runny noses. No physical reaction at all.

And it was at that point I thought, my God, I'm a successful hypnotist.

The audience didn't know whether to laugh or what. They were being everything from astounded, through amazed and of course amused.

And I'd just met their subconscious mind and witnessed the power of the subconscious to override their natural physiological and deeply embedded reaction to the point where they could do something normally impossible.

So that evening stage hypnosis taught me that the subconscious mind creates its own reality and that reality can be…

Well, we could use the word manipulated, but a lot of people get the wrong idea if we do, so let's say *subconsciously and psychologically directed.*

But your subconscious mind is not totally unlimited obviously because if you hypnotise people and tell them that they can fly; well it's quite funny watching them try to take off.

So, that was a point of success for me, using a skill that actually I have always had, the skill of suggestion, and direction to achieve what I set out to do.

A Subconscious Skill Success ;-)

What's going on?

Jane: So, Jon, are there any specific areas for
         our readers where you can see where
         things are going to get shaken up, have a
         major impact or even shape the future?

Jon: Well, you know, communication's stayed
         the same but the way we communicate
         has changed dramatically. And it affects
         us subconsciously now more than ever.

         There's a huge drive to capture people's
         attention but, it's what sneaks in around
         our conscious that makes the most
         difference.

         In my lifetime, it's gone from two tins
         strung together with a piece of string and
         holding that very tight to your ear,
         through battery walkie talkies right the
         way through to now, where you can have

a video conversation with somebody on the other side of the world instantly on a watch!

Just the other day I was coaching a client from New Zealand, and I'm here at home in the English Riviera.

Obviously the actual conversation, the actual talking, the actual sharing of knowledge and sharing of meaning is the same as it's been since language was invented.

So, I think the thing that's going to make the most change is the format of conversation rather than conversation itself.

Video is very important because the smile is still a smile and a laugh is still a laugh.

I don't think the conversation itself changes. Humans change and cultures change and the meaning and understanding of specific words change but communication pretty much stays ... well it stays pretty much the same.

There's going to be a lot of changes in the future as one generation grows up and blames the previous generation for all its ills and, hopefully, realises that it's going to be responsible for the next generation's problems as far as they're concerned.

I'm a baby boomer and if you're a millennial that means it's all my fault and if you're an X gen, it's all your fault.

That's the adult child part of our society that changes with the times. But, we're talking here about subconscious communication skills which actually works pretty much the same.

The Conscious is inclined to blame the Subconscious and the reverse is true.

However the conscious is as they say in neuroscience, 'Plastic'. Obviously it's not, it's a grungy grey slippy organ made of mostly meat, but its infrastructure can be adjusted to restructure connections that retain different information.

23

However as far as we can tell, your SUBconscious is what you are born with - and pretty much what you'll die with when it comes to traits, tendencies, talents and basic behavioural response patterns. And there's a lot of those. Gordon Allport, a pioneering psychologist, actually came up with a list of around 4,000.

A lot of the process we call the Subconscious is innate. it's onboard, hard wired, firmware. It can and probably will change over a lifetime but as recent studies have shown, only very subtly.

You can observe this yourself if you get a group of infants, a group of little babies that are say... under the age of six or seven months old, it doesn't matter where you get them from in the human world, and you put them all in a group you'll be able to see communication skills going on even at the age of seven or eight months.

Just one of our innate abilities, and you'll also see their subconscious style.

Those skills pass from one human being to another and they haven't changed yet because they haven't been super imposed with the cognitive stuff.

And that's where the apparent big changes come from, when the natural subconscious way to communicate is being superseded by the socially based conscious, by the cognitive stuff.

For this book, I think we need to stop worrying about the conscious communication skills that we're told that we've got to have, and start thinking about letting our subconscious mind just connect.

SubSkills and Emotions

Jane: So, what is the impact of successfully using our subconscious skills on people's emotions?

Jon: Well, you know, emotion is a strange thing. Emotions are usually reactions, they're not precursors, so something happens to us around this, we see something or we imagine something and we react to that.

          When you get good at your subconscious skills, you start to reason subconsciously, and I know that's going against the general understanding of the subconscious but I'll explain more about that later on.

So, the subconscious response, without very much reason, when it doesn't reason things through, might go something like this.

Something happens that you find distasteful, you might get angry or scared about that or anxious about it or whatever, without really thinking about it, so in an internal conversation you might say, "Do I want this? Do I want this emotion? Do I want this reaction?"

If not, you may be able to consciously override and control the reaction, but the emotion and all its chemo-electrical responses in your brain will still be there underneath everything.

In SubSkills it's not about being able to overcome emotions or control emotions, it's simply being able to *choose* emotions.

For instance, if you're looking at an emotion you're having because something's going on over there, if you ask yourself the question, "do I want this?" And you say "no", well, leave it alone then, go away, go away from it, move away from it, think about something else, imagine something else, go somewhere else.

Don't try and control, simply go away.

People think that this is really hard, that you really can't do it. Obviously, if you're in a traumatic situation or a traumatic occurrence, say, I don't know, a fire or a volcano erupting or something like that, the sensible response subconsciously, ***and*** consciously, is to run away from it.

And I know you're told to stick and face your fear and face everything else, but the sensible thing and the obvious thing is to run away from it and then think about it, and then get a handle on the emotions and say, "well, do I want these emotions? And are these emotions useful to me? Should I be doing that?"

So, it's sort of like one of the big things when you get good at this, and we'll explain how a little bit later on, and how to choose your moods and how to choose your emotions, but one of the big things that you're going to get out of this is that you'll be able to say, turn fear into excitement.

It's proven scientifically that if you just think of fear as excitement, the chemical reaction inside your brain changes a tiny amount, and as soon as the chemical reaction inside your brain changes, then those emotions change and you've got a reason and that's just by not trying to stop the emotion, but by *changing the way that you see the emotion,* and *changing the way that you feel about the emotion.* Not fighting it or changing it but just interpreting it differently.

You're still feeling exactly the same thing neurologically and physically but the response changes.

I always used to do this; when I was talking to classes about anxiety, I always used to say, right, we talk about panic and anxiety for ten minutes, and then I'll say, "Right, what am I describing? Your breathing gets shorter and shallower, you begin to sweat, your muscles begin to almost respond on their own and tense and involuntarily spasm.

Your heart rate rises and you start to get really tense and…"

The arms in the class would shoot up and everybody would say, **panic attack**, **panic attack**.

Actually I'm describing something that's almost exactly the same physiologically but it's different psychologically.

I'm describing an orgasm!

So, having the point where we're increasing our subconscious skills will give us more, not control, but more understanding and more connection with our emotions.

That results in more direction - a bit like being our own Spielberg.

Jane: So that we react differently.

Jon: So that we react more productively, yes.

Jane: So that's what you're changing, it's the
        reaction rather than the mood or ...

Jon: Changing the *impact* of the reaction. Yes.

Meditation And Therapy Theory

Jane: We always wonder if there are alternatives to the things that we talk about and the things that we think about.

So, we know your approach to subconscious skills is entirely different from the majority of approaches out there, but what are the alternatives? What do we need to be aware of?

Jon: Okay, let's look at these.

When you look into the 'religion' of personal development and skills for success, there's a lot of talk about positive thinking, meditation and therapeutic techniques...

All of which can be proven to 'work' for some of the people for some of the time.

I think a lot of that stuff works because the person doing it feels a bit better wielding a tool he's seen the guru getting results with, and then the respondents subconscious is going along with that influencer's confident approach, which of course we are all attracted to.

There's no doubt meditative states can over time bring about and support calmer mindsets. But it takes time and if we're in the throws of trauma it's not always available to us when we need it.

As a pragmatic guy I'm a bit agnostic when it comes to the positive thinking thing. I think Productive beats Positive hands down and no, I don't think the two are the same at all.

You can actually be very productive in the middle of being angry. I booked my first show after my mentor told me I'd never be a stage hypnotist as long as I had

a hole in my arse. That put me in a "I'll
show you!" mindset.

And positive doesn't always bring about
the desired result, as the late Stella Young
says in her Ted talk '**I'm not your
inspiration**'

*"I really think that this lie that we've been sold
about disability is the greatest injustice. It makes
life hard for us. And that quote, 'The only
disability in life is a bad attitude,' the reason
that that's bullshit is because it's just not true,
because of the social model of disability. No
amount of smiling at a flight of stairs has ever
made it turn into a ramp. Never. (Laughter)
(Applause). Smiling at a television screen isn't
going to make closed captions appear for people
who are deaf. No amount of standing in the
middle of a bookshop and radiating a positive
attitude is going to turn all those books into
braille. It's just not going to happen."*

Jane: So, you mentioned persuasion and also
        you mentioned influence. What for you is
        the difference between the two, between
        influence and persuasion?

Jon: For me there's a very definite difference.

People say to me all the time, there is no
difference, that persuasion is influence
and influence is persuasion, but I disagree
on a couple of levels.

I'm not a lexicographer or a linguist or
anything like that but I do know one
thing, that is, that generally speaking,
dictionaries are bloody good books
because they give you the vast agreed
understanding of a word, and, when you
read what persuasion is in the dictionary,
it's different from influence.

So, looking them up....

Persuasion: the action or fact of persuading
somebody or being persuaded to do or
believe something.
A belief or set of beliefs, especially
religious or political ones.

Whereas;

Influence: is the capacity to have an affect on the
character development or behaviour of
someone or something or the affect itself
to have an influence on.

So, as far as I'm concerned, and I think it's fairly safe that I'm backed up by most dictionaries.

Which I know is ignored most of the time and I do understand that words have an organic changing nature, and I come from a time when cool meant slightly less warm, but, taking the dictionary meanings aside, the way I explain the difference between persuasion and influence is:

Persuasion is when you have something you want somebody else to want, and you have to suggest to them that it's a great idea to have that, remove their objections and then manipulate them into wanting the thing enough to actually take it from you, to take part in the exchange.

Influence is entirely different. Influencers are people that others want to be, they want to follow them. They have ideas, they have conceptions, they have beliefs that others want to follow, when they don't need to be persuaded. They look at the thing the influencer has and they say, hey, that's good, I want that, rather than saying, what's that? Should I have that or not? Well, I'll persuade you to have it.

I can do both. I can do the persuasion.

I was a stage hypnotist for more years than you can swing a watch at, but there again, I always taught in stage hypnosis, the reason that we only get 12 people on stage out of an audience of 2000, or maybe we get 30 or 40 people, depending on how hard you want to work, but when you're doing that, it looks like you're persuading people to come up on stage.

You're not persuading anybody because they've already made their minds up before they even came in the room... It's more influence than it is persuasion.

That's one thing that you've got to teach people all the time is be an influencer, don't be a persuader because an influencer is about who and what you are and a persuader is about what you want people to want. Because you're who you are and what you are and people want to join, they want to learn, they want to take the knowledge, they want to come on board into your, hate these terms but they're there, into your tribe, your community, your gang, whatever you want to call it, and they want to come in and follow you and find out what you know and what your experience is.

It's much easier to be an influencer than it is to be a persuader because all you've got to do as far as sub-skills is concerned, as far as subconscious skills are concerned, is be you and be you as big as you can be. So, it's a lot easier to be an influencer than a persuader.

Jane: So what about Therapy as an alternative approach to getting more success?

Jon: (Sighs). Trouble with therapy is that the simple meaning of the word requires anybody wanting, needing or getting it, to be sick. To, at the very least see themselves as sick, ill, damaged…

This is very often just not a great place to start from.

I get that if you've had a traumatic experience you can see the result as damage, I've had 15 operations, including one on my heart, and 35 fractures and have got a couple of pounds of internal scaffolding in my thigh and set alarms off in airports but, I'm not currently ill or sick.

There are people who are and that's fine, but a lot of what is viewed as illness just isn't.

Stress, the internal conflict between the conscious and subconscious processes obviously causes symptoms that look like a disease, but there's no virus, no bacteria, no injury involved.

And the cure of the cause is usually just getting the two bits of your being to play nicely together and co-operate.

Jane: To reprogram our brain?

Jon: Absolutely not. The brain isn't a computer. I know that's the common analogy but it's a misnomer. The brain is a lump of flesh. It's organic and in constant response mode, but it's also self aware, something A.I., will hopefully never be able to be.

The subconscious is probably much more than just a result of the brain, although it certainly uses the thinking mechanism, but it can't be programmed as such. It has being in the same way as the conscious.

Okay so it probably isn't an entirely separate entity or personality, in fact it IS our personality, and it won't be told, led or programmed. And at least half of it is hard wired DNA, as far as talent, traits, tendencies are concerned. That's why we can profile it, check out the free MindSTYLEapp.com.

However you can co-operate with the process, guide the process, gently shove it on the right path or cajole and coax it to follow what it does best, to the advantage of your *whole self*.

Meet Your Subconscious

Jane: Okay Jon, so you're on record as saying that the subconscious process can be seen as a bright 9 to 10 year old child. Can you explain that for us please?

Jon: Sure.

Imagine a human being was a car...

In this case it's being driven by Peter, it could be being driven by Petunia or Pauline but in this case it's Peter.

Peter knows where the car is pointed and he has learnt the skills to drive it there.

Peter is the conscious brain, and is mature enough to understand that there's social rules, and he's had enough experience to know how far to bend those and not get into trouble or to cause a smash or a crash.

His car is pretty much where it should be on the road surrounded by slower, faster, bigger and smaller vehicles, and it's a not too expensive, not too cheap car, that doesn't do too much damage to the world, or to Peter's pocket, and it can go faster if he chooses.

Peter know's where his car is pointed.

He's not absolutely positive what will be there when he gets there, but he's checked the internet site and brochures. He's spoken to a few people who've been there, admittedly a few years ago and for varying reasons from different directions, however, he's got a pretty good idea it will be worth the trip which should be pleasant and profitable, and, according to google maps, without too many holdups or diversions.

If you were passing Peter and glanced across you'd see a pretty much peaceful and passive Peter

But.

Peter's car has back seats.

In one of those back seats, behind Peter's, behind the privacy glass, which is why you didn't see the nose thumbing, tongue out, sits Paul.

Meet Your Subconscious

Paul or Penny or Pat, but in this case Paul, is somewhere between 9 and 10 years old.

Paul may want to go where Peter's going because he likes the car, sometimes.

He really likes it when he's allowed to sit in the front seat next to Peter pressing buttons and turning the radio up - or down, or on to his favourite shows, and opening the window and twiddling with...

But mostly, he's in the back seat.

Now unlike the radio Paul didn't come with a volume control or off switch.

Paul did however come with loads of attention getting skills designed to help Paul get what Paul wants and needs.

Sometimes those give Peter what he wants and needs, and then everything is perfect, and a lot of the time... it's not really.

Paul doesn't really see where the car is pointed, even when he's in the front because forward, or backwards, isn't where he's looking.

Paul is pointed at a place Paul imagines is the place he wants to be, and Paul doesn't get why he isn't 'there yet'.

"Are we there yet?" is Paul's main mantra and, 'are we there yet?', is often punctuated by, "Will there be ice-cream? I want ice-cream! Is that a rabbit? Can we play Eye-Spy? I need a pee... Can we have a rabbit? Will there be ice-cream? I think I feel sick… Are we there yet?"

And unfortunately the back-seat isn't soundproofed or in a different parallel universe so Peter is always aware of Paul no matter what.

And, sooner or later Peter will stop to buy ice-cream, play eye-spy, buy a rabbit or take that short cut or put the pedal to the metal to get there faster; even though Peter knows if he gets caught he'll end up with points on his licence and a longer trip overall. . . or even worse...

Inside *all of us* there is a 'Paul' process that affects all of our decisions and dictates most of our responses, relationships, reactions, beliefs and behaviours.

It's emotional, playful, imaginative, and the basis of our personality and the home of our natural talents, tendencies, traits and tastes.

Probably based around our oldest paleo-mammalian brain the *limbic system,* what some people call a monkey brain or even way more off the truth, the reptilian brain, it's pretty much set up by the time we hit pre-puberty around 9 years six months old.

And although it can be influenced, like any 9 year old, it isn't going to do *anything* we want it to, if we try to force it.

We call this process, or entity if you prefer, our Mind or Subconscious.

It really is who we are, and why we are us.

The world is protected from it most of the time because our social, logical, reasonable and constantly maturing cerebral cortex brain, our conscious, is a little like an adult driving a car.

And just like the adult and child, the brain's main job is to direct and drive while at the same time trying to tell the child why it's not there yet, and to be quiet please, and to explain to the world why that didn't work. . .

Emilé Coué, author of the line, 'every day and every way I'm getting better and better', called them the Imagination (child), and Intellect (adult), and in his 1921 short and insightful book on how to master the subconscious he said, "If there's a conflict between the imagination and intellect, the imagination always wins."

Anyone who's ever been a parent of a bright 9 year old, knows that the pre-pubescent child is pretty much why they do what they do and the child usually wins.

Oh yes they do - go on - be honest.

Jane: Well yes, one way or another they do.

Jon   Your subconscious has built in skills to get what it wants. Survival and communication skills that go beyond and before mere logical language, they are hard wired in at birth.

The child will execute natural techniques to wheedle the ice-cream, and it's happiness expressed in chemicals like dopamine and endorphins, noradrenaline, serotonin, is the adults reward, even if it makes the kid explode.

Maturing and growing up, learning to drive, overrides those simple skills with more complex social rules and regulations, so you forget how to *just get* what you want and need, and we also forget how to *just give* what others want and need.

Of course, your subconscious skills are still there, and when you let Paul in the front seat, and this time make everything a game and allow Paul to press the right buttons and twiddle the best knobs, then the results are the best rewards.

Obviously that's a metaphor to explain the relationship with the conscious and subconscious process.

Actually the subconscious - and this is lay science so if you're a neurologist you'll have to forgive me - is a collection of thought processes. A web of response and reaction and recall mechanisms in our brain we can better think of as our minds.

Obviously if we look at it purely bio-mechanically then one thought looks pretty much like any other. All processes appear the same. Love, hate, anger, fear, lust, are all just chemical and electrical connections between cells.

I think it's a useful model to think of the conscious and subconscious as the Brain and the Mind and when we do that we get this…

BRAIN:

The Conscious organised organ used to think with. It is logical and serious and matures with age. Is reality based Organic organ.

MIND:

The Subconscious. The process of thinking which is creative, emotive, illogical and often childlike in its simplicity. It may be a separate entity or the produce of a functioning cognitive system. Decides and judges from an internalised perception of reality.

Emile Coué, author of the mantra-like conscious autosuggestion, "Every day, in every way, I'm getting better and better", called them the Intellect and the Imagination, and went on to make the observation that when in conflict, the Imagination always wins.

He wasn't wrong.

Get the best from this book

Jane: So, if subconscious success is the answer, what do success seeking professional communicators need to know? And what's the right mind set or physical state for them to be in when it comes to getting started with subconscious skills to get the most out of what's coming next and how do we get there?

Jon: Say somebody's reading this book or somebody's interested in what we're saying here right now, what you've got to do is first think what you want subconsciously.

          I know there's lots of goal setting and there's lots of people who would say, what shape is your success going to be?

What are your goals going to be? They've got to be smart. You've got to think big and another person will say, oh, you've got to dream massively and all that.

Have a conversation, have a chat with your best friend and sometimes your worst enemy, but basically, this is a time when you just have a talk to yourself.

Now, people are told, we're told from childhood that talking to ourselves is the first sign of insanity which is ridiculous because everybody talks to themselves, everybody berates themselves when they do something stupid or something naughty. Everybody says, I did well there, didn't I? When they've done something that's really great and that feels good.

So, we talk to ourselves all the time anyway.

What I want you to do if you're listening or reading this just stop and have a think what you want subconsciously.

Have a chat with yourself. Say to the subconscious, right, okay, let's play a game. I'm going to play the game of what do I want. So, here's one voice and here's another voice. So, this first voice says what do I want? "Doughnuts". Now, that was the first thing that came into my mind and I haven't had doughnuts in years, but it was the first thing that came out of my mind.

What do I want? Now, this is a little bit word association, but it's a game. It's a little game that you can play and I want you to start playing it and I want you to start playing it all the time, because if you think, right, okay, I'm going networking tomorrow, what do I want? Three new friends, and three new connections.

What do I want? A bright pink Ferrari.

What do I want? Pencils.

What do I want? Book signing.

What do I want? JV partner.

What do I want?

Now, this is literally me doing this right here and now. Some of the things that are coming out of my subconscious mind are making sense and some of the things aren't.

If I look at it cognitively, some of this is cognitive, some of it is obviously my logical conscious.

Oh, I'm going networking, I need a joint venture partner, a JV partner, but looking at it, the thing that strikes me even more had I written those down, I'm just remembering them now, but had I written them down, one of the most surprising things I think is *three new friends*. Not one, not two but three new friends.

People I can *call* friends.

Now, friends are important because friends, as Facebook will tell you, friends are way more important than connections, yeah? That's why people have a completely different mindset on

Facebook than they do on LinkedIn. I want three new friends because friends recommend you, friends like the stuff you like, friends want to come on your journey with you.

So, that's a simple little game that you can play before you get into the steps and before you get into the skills themselves.

The skills, I've got to warn you, the skills are going to be fairly random, they're not in any particular order, they're certainly not strategic, but you can take those skills and put them into a strategic order to help **you** remember them if you want to.

They're probably in the order that *my* subconscious mind prefers to use them in and think about them, because I'm fairly subconscious anyway, so I want you to get subconscious.

The little 'what do I want game' if you play it very, very quickly, and write down all the things that you want, and write down everything that comes into your mind, don't judge it.

I know that some of it is going to be completely off the board and some of it's going to be rude, some of it's going to be impossible, some of it's going to be highly unlikely, but I'm a bit of an agnostic when it comes to the religion of personal development and I don't advocate that anything you can imagine you can have, because I think if you can have anything you can imagine, then the first thing you'd need is a new imagination because I can imagine being a spider on mars and that's highly unlikely being on mars or being a spider for that matter, but you can do this.

Say to yourself Jane, "what do I want".

Jane: What do I want?

Jon: And then give me a list of the things that come out of your mind. Now, let's make it specific. You're helping me develop this book, so what do you want for the book. Say "what do I want?" and then just say the first five things that come into your head. Very quickly.

Jane: Lots of readers.

Jon: That's a bit too Conscious. What do you want? What do I want? What do I want? What do I want? Keep saying that until something unusual comes to mind, quickly.

Jane: Successful book.

Jon: Successful book. Again too conscious.

Jane: I don't know. All I can think of at the moment is a pink Ferrari!

Jon: Okay I don't know. What do I want? *I don't know.* That is not a bad answer then in this situation, it's an honest one.

Jane: Okay.

Jon: Yeah. That is not a bad answer. I don't know **yet**. Okay?

Jane: Okay.

Jon: So then, you think, well, it's not your book, is it? But then you think, okay, the next situation, what do I want? What do I want? What do I want? What do I want? Until you get to the point where you're getting answers that make emotional sense to you.

Jane: Okay, I'll try it another time.

Jon: Yeah? Okay. Now, the other thing is, that I said turn this into a game, if you turn it into a game, it makes it fun because the subconscious mind is a bright nine year old. I'll explain that in a little while. But, turn it into a game.

          The other thing I want to really get here, what you need to do, is experiment and the beauty of experimentation is you cannot lose.

          You can't lose an experiment because whatever the result is, is the result of the experiment.

          If you're experimenting with something, if you're saying to your subconscious mind, let's experiment with this, you try it and whatever happens is what happens, then you decide whether that was productive or unproductive. But, the result is always the result. There's no win or lose with experimentation. Just try it because you don't know whether anything will work unless you try it.

Feed Your Brain

Jane: Okay and on to the strategies, the first of which in the list you gave me is **Feed Your Brain**. So is this going to be about diet and things like carrots help you see better?

Jon: No. There's loads of great books about nutrition and that is a huge field. And it isn't about learning loads either because that just uses the brain, it doesn't feed it.

No, as we've already touched on, the brain is an organ. It relies on energy, as does everything, and as such can benefit in the short term by simply giving it more fuel to burn.

The best fuel is of course oxygen.

The Human Cognitive Neuroscience unit at the University of Northumbria are being widely quoted for their findings that people taking recreational oxygen have better test results than those who didn't.

I'm no expert on recreational oxygen but am aware that there's quite a bit of the stuff about anyway, without buying it in cans, even in the smoggiest of city centres.

I do know for sure that breathing in deeply for a count of 8, holding it for a count of 5, and breathing out for a count of 8 will get lots more oxygen into your blood and your brain.

Do that three or four times before you are going to do something where you know you'll be relying on your imagination, your response system, your emotions, or any time where you think or feel you may be a bit stressed and your brain will simply work better.

And while your Mind may not be your Brain, it uses it for sure. So a quick energy fix won't hurt anything.

A drink of water also goes a long way to fire the old grey cells.

Panting does the same, so any intensive exercise that makes you pant and your heart race will energise everything.

However MY favourite way of deep breathing and moving quickly on to the next strategy is that of laughter.

Watch a quick youtube video, read a joke, or even just remember the last time you LOLed at something and get a good guffaw going.

We've all heard of laughter yoga and it works to super breath and pant as well as firing endorphins and the all important neurotransmitters. Which we'll talk about next...

Using Your Dopamine Factor

Jane: Okay, so neurotransmitters.. do tell...

Jon: Well there are about 5 to 7 well known
        chemicals that basically make the
        connections between cells when we think.

        If you're not a chemist best to think of
        them as flags that signal information
        from one cell to another.

        They have different chemical structures
        and are produced as the response to
        different events. It's all extremely
        complicated and it's happening right now
        inside your brain.

        ALL we need to know for the purpose of
        this strategy though, is that there is one
        of these bio-chemicals involved
        specifically with our learning, our
        motivation and our pleasure called
        Dopamine.

        Neuroscience and pharmacology is
        currently of the opinion that Dopamine
        fires what they call motivational salience.
        In other words it decides our behaviour

towards or away from a particular object, perceived event, or outcome.

Good or bad.

The popular un-researched idea used to think of Dopamine as the *pleasure drug*. Only there to make us feel great, which with other NT's, like Serotonin, it can do.

It is certainly more abundant when we are expecting something good And there's loads of evidence that there's more dopamine about when we have got to the point when that event or experience is causing us to respond with laughter.

Now apart from taking a Dopamine tablet, which has been tested for Parkinson's disease and is looking to be very useful, you'll need to use your own chemical factories to produce the stuff. And when you do you'll learn faster and retain more.

It's for that reason, what I call the Dopamine Factor, that mostly we can recall the lessons we learnt in the playground at school than we can the classroom.

Jane: I see but don't a lot of people have less than happy memories of playgrounds?

Jon: Yes, but Dopamine is produced as well when we're experiencing something we need to move away from, and not towards.

That's why being scared produces the effect of rapid learning and why phobias are produced almost instantly. Neurotransmitters helping us to learn to avoid the painful.

So you can use the **Dopamine Factor strategy** by *scaring* yourself stupid, but you might find making what you are doing as much *fun* as possible, to be the better approach.

And if you're learning something that's boring or tedious, you can still get it in faster and better if you're focused on the enjoyable conclusion. So imagine being able to do something really enjoyable in the future, even if that's just finishing the learning...

Games and Experiments

Jane: So tell us more about games…

Jon: Now we've already said that a great way
        of looking at your subconscious is as a
        bright nine to ten year old child.

        That's hard wired and never changes after
        9 - 10 years old.

        And let's face it when we were nine and a
        half we loved to play didn't we? We learnt
        from it. ALL animals learn from games
        and play.

        We start off of course playing without
        rules. We just play. We run around and
        climb coal mine slag heaps, and run and
        jump off the top, sliding down the loose
        shale and amazingly don't get buried alive.

        Or we kick a ball against a wall for hours
        or until our Dad shouts, "Our Jon, stop
        banging that bloody ball!"

        Sorry went off a bit there… maybe that
        was just me.

Nowadays of course we crush candy's or run around virtual worlds for two weeks in the pursuit of doing a victory dance for slaughtering as many foes as possible.

We play, because playing is fun and the part of us that doesn't care that it's a huge time sapping exercise, has the maturity of a child.

Now we can fight this of course. We can *add rules, limits, and guilt* to stop us doing it, but we *still* want to play.

In fact in westernised society we gravitate more towards games than anything else. It's what we do when we go on vacation. It's mostly what we do with our children. And even if we're not taking part ourselves we happily go and pay to watch others playing.

Leisure time very often involves games and play in the forms of sports, theatre, movies, television, even business can be seen as a game… which of course it should.

Let's face it a lot of our exercise is really nothing more than a game, or could be turned into a game.

Games have become so important we even turn them into professions that afford almost as much gravitas as wars, and sometimes, with almost less bloodshed.

So, *turning tasks into games* helps to make doing them more appealing to our subconscious.

Or even taking game breaks, just like we allow our children to do, can help alleviate boredom.

Jane: Using the 50 minute rule?

Jon: Yes why not? There's good evidence that 50 minutes is the longest the human brain can totally focus on something without a break.

I think that's true, and probably the reason for our bodies wanting to fidget on long drives.

71

Thing is, if you are also subconsciously looking forward to the break, you've guessed it, looking forward to a pleasurable event fires dopamine, you actually work better.

So *use your subconscious* to maybe throw a ball up the wall and catch it until your boss, partner or kids yell, "Oi, stop banging that bloody ball!"

Experiments are great as well. It's impossible for an experiment to actually fail.

Whatever you end up with is the result.

It may not be the result you were expecting or hoping for. It may be surprising or even shocking, but, it's just the result.

Thinking that what you are doing is an experiment, has a wonderful effect subconscious success wise. It means you get more of it.

I know that appears to go against most of the goal setting exact intent stuff out there, but our subconscious Mind actually doesn't donate goal stuff all that well. Unless the goals are to feel something or experience something.

That's why the best goal setting systems *add as much emotion* to the set goal as possible.

And we should go for the emotive experiment. '*How will this make me feel?*' is a better place to start than '*this will make me feel like this…*'

The old saying, '*you get what you expect*' is of course true. So if you're always expecting the result, you'll always see a lot more success.

Listen Like A Leader

Jane: Listen like a leader. What is this skill and
        how do you do it?

Jon: I used to, in my other book, '**How To
        Make Friends With Yourself and
        Influence People**', as part of the
        training course that I run that the book's
        a transcript of, we do a thing called
        '**Parrot Rapport**', which is just a simple,
        easy way of keeping a conversation going
        and making that person feel important.

        Now, in his book, '*How to win friends and
        influence people*', Dale Carnegie said, "it's
        important that you make people feel
        important" and that's what leaders do.

        Leaders make people feel important, but
        more importantly, and this is a realisation
        I've got from training more and more
        people, and coaching more and more
        people in this, I won't say that I've trained
        and coached... say politicians, because
        there are things like non-disclosure
        documents that restrict what you can say

and what you can't say fairly tightly. So I won't say that I've ever done that.

But one of the points of using methods like this is that it ***makes*** you listen. And when you ***actually listen*** then you start to subconsciously change your emotions, change your mood, and you subconsciously go with the flow better.

And rapport ... and I'll say this again and again, rapport is about resonating with the person that you're with. It's got nothing to do with trust, or like, or anything like that. It's not even that person feels comfortable with you.

Rapport is *all* about moving toward the same or very similar reward. I'm doing my thing; you're doing your thing and we can be in rapport if I want to sell, and you want to buy.

Football supporters either end of the stadium are in rapport, they both want the other team to lose.

Now one of the easiest ways of entering rapport is for me to find out what you're actually talking about, and move towards that with you.

And the only way I can find out what you're actually talking about is to **listen like a leader**. And that doesn't mean that I'm going to take over the conversation at any point or point it to wherever I want it to go, *yet*.

It means I'm totally involved in what you are saying.

There's a simple, easy little trick that you can use to do this. And by trick, I don't mean anything duplicitous; I don't mean anything sneaky or, you know, wrong or bad. By trick, I mean a skilful way of doing this.

How you do it skilfully; is to listen, and then to repeat part of what's been said.

So let's do this.

Jane, we've just met! What are you here for?

Jane: Well I'm here to interview you for a book...

Jon: To Interview me?

Jane: Yes... Well I suppose it's more like prompting or even leading...

Jon: So, in this case I repeat the *second thing* that was said to me back to you, because that felt important. And if that feels like it's coming from you from a deep place.

        I also add a *question mark* at the end so you almost automatically expand on it. And that also puts it in my head because - well it's a game. Or an experiment if you like...

        So to do this and sort of calibrate what's important to you, and so should be to me, I tune in to my own subconscious and say, "right, okay, I'm going to listen, but I'm going to *feel* as well."

And I'm *not* listening for sub-modalities, I'm *not* listening for word patterns, I'm *not* listening for anything that's complex or complicated. I'm feeling and listening for what's important and that makes it more subconscious than conscious and therefore more subskill.

That way we keep everything simple.

What I am doing is listening for the bits that you seem to *enjoy* giving me most. I'm listening for the bits where you *smile most*. I'm listening for the bits when you get me going. But I'm listening to the whole thing, because I don't know which bits I'm going to use. So I'm going to listen to the whole thing.

You say a sentence or a paragraph. And you say something that I can feed back to you. Now if you said, well, I like doing this or I want to do that, then I might say, oh, so you like doing this? And I'll put a big question mark on the end of it.

Now say you've just said, I like doing this. And I picked up on "I *like* doing this." Not I do that.

Do you understand where I'm going with this? I'm picking up the "I *like* to do this," and I'm watching how you are, and I'm observing how you are and I'm *tuning into your emotions*. And I'm not doing anything deliberately. I'm letting my subconscious mind guide me on the bits that I'm going to repeat because I know it's good at this. Then the only conscious thing I need to do is to put a big question on it.

Now this isn't new, you've been doing it your whole life. It's how you learnt to speak, how you learnt to do most things.

If you watch children talking, they repeat what's being said to them with a question mark on the end of it, to see if they got it right. To see if they've understood it right. That's how we learn language. That's how everybody learns language.

Do it. Watch kids speaking and notice how your grandchildren, when you're telling them something, will repeat bits of it back to you with a question mark on the end just to make sure that they got that right. Yes?

And that goes on until we're ... you know, it should go on forever, but unfortunately it doesn't; we get to the point where we think we don't need to learn anymore or worse we try to get clever and make everything conscious.

So that goes on into our teenage years, because that's the point where we think we know it all and intellect takes over.

So listening like a leader is about listening and giving some of that back. It takes practise. All subconscious skills take practise because you haven't done it since you were five.

Jane: Right.

Jon: Because you have stopped doing it. Is that clear?

Jane: So I haven't really done it since I was five?

Jon: No. No, you haven't used subconscious skills in the way that you're going to for most of your grownup childhood. And I'm calling it the grownup childhood because when people, instead of getting all excited because you just repeated something to them, actually told you to shut up because you weren't supposed to be saying that then and there. And that's when we start to get taught. It's when we start to get educated, and that's when everything goes wrong.

So, listening like a leader is about listening to what's being said to the point where you know and understand what is turning that person's oars, what's floating that person's boat, and giving that back to them. But *verifying* that you heard it with a question mark. This has the effect on the person that you're listening to ... they're thinking, 'my god she's actually listening', and they're doing *that* subconsciously!

But here's the big thing. It stops you thinking about what you've got to say next.

It stops you thinking about how do I manipulate this person.

It stops you thinking about what's my pitch.

It stops you thinking about what am I going to say, what's my part in this conversation.

And you get more and more into, and out of, the conversation.

And that's what leaders do. Leaders don't lead a conversation.

Leaders listen.

Manifest a Miracle Memory

Jane: As we get older memory becomes a problem for very many people doesn't it? What can we do subconsciously, using our imagination, to remember things better?

Jon: You can manifest, that just means to make a list of something, but it also got related to the 'unconscious' process of dreaming in one of Freud's theories around dreaming.

    Many, many years ago I was doing some training with a guy called Wilf Proudfoot at his hypnosis training academy in Scarborough. It was back in the the '80s; I'm very old.

    Wilf was teaching us about how to create a wonderful place in our imagination and to use this to gather energy, to focus, and everything like that.

    And as part of becoming a stage hypnotist and a mentalist, memory tricks and memory things are important to you.

You need to remember stuff. Not just scripts and tricks and effects and presentations, you also need to remember the person's name when they come up on stage.

You need to remember where you put things, which pocket has got the envelope in.

And there are those who with practice and a device such as mnemonics or a memory mansion have developed whole memory acts, and no doubt have won the odd game or quiz show.

People think, oh, that looks easy. It's not, actually. It's quite complex and complicated and requires constant practice… and there are some of us of course who just cheat.

But here's the thing with a miracle memory. We're not talking about a forever memory. And we're not talking about a photographic memory. Because most of the mnemonic things, most of the memory systems to develop a fantastic, brilliant memory, are long-term memory stuff.

Talking about it here on a subconscious level and our subconscious skills, we're not really that interested or bothered in a long-term memory. Because most people have got wonderful long-term memories.

Most people can remember being kids. Even people our age, baby boomers, can remember being children. But it's not detailed. And the reason it's not detailed is your mind only keeps hold of the very strong patterns. And those strong patterns are the ones that were developed when you got the most dopamine on board.

And as we've said dopamine is a neurotransmitter. Think of it like oil in a car engine. It's there to make the neurone connections. And the connections that you make in your brain, it's there to make them easier and stronger. The electro-chemical signals can pass through the synapses faster and easier and make stronger connections if there's dopamine on board. The less dopamine, the less you remember. The more dopamine, the more you remember.

Dopamine is built up really through excitement, through hope. I'm moving towards this, I'm enjoying this, I'm going towards this. But what a lot of people don't know is that dopamine is also present when you're scared shitless. Dopamine's also present when lots of noradrenaline's about. When you are your most emotional.

The **dopamine factor** is important in developing a miracle memory. And we call it miracle memory, but like most miracles it only happens once and it only happens for a short time. So you don't have to over-concentrate on this. Just add something emotional, or **just imagine something that makes you smile attached to the event or detail you need to recall.**

This creates a pattern of connections we call memory. It's like having Instagram in your head. A series of photos, a snapshot or a short video.

Jane: In some ways that's what you're building up in your mind ...

Jon: Yes, you're building up an image. You're building up a picture.

Jane: ... a mental map. so is there a simple way to do this?

Jon: When I started teaching hypnosis, I wanted people to remember what I was teaching them, so we developed a mnemonic system we called, HAL, or Hypnotically Accelerated Learning.

It quickly became obvious that this works without any need for trance or swinging watches, and in fact, it often works better when your conscious is actually observing what it is you are imagining.

First ask your subconscious to create a perfect place inside your mind. It can be anywhere, any time, anything in or out of the universe.

87

A place that is wonderful and nice and marvellous.

And if you don't visualise, you can just describe this place to yourself. You can use a story instead of visualisation.

And then bring in to that place a container or a receptacle. Doesn't matter what that is just allow the subconscious to choose.

We've had all sorts reported. Once a student said they imagined a Canal Narrow Boat for instance that their Mind sank so it couldn't float away.

Now you have to trust that the process is exactly right for you whatever comes up go with it without question. A lot of mnemonic systems tell you what to imagine. Problem with that is that it's making the process almost conscious and that brings an edge of logical doubt we don't need or want.

So if we want to remember, let's keep things as Subconscious as possible.

Now you bring into your subconscious mind a *perfect place*, you bring into your imagination, a *container*, a *receptacle*, something you can put something in.

You can put something in something fairly solid as it can be hollow, or whatever. It doesn't matter. Then quite simply ask your subconscious to put everything you *want to remember* in that thing.

And as soon as you turn that memory into a specific thing, when you come to recall it *your mind only has to remember the model that is the container.* Everything else is 'attached' to that.

You can also then forget to remember as it's not remembering, it's creating the memory model, and that's much easier than trying to 'remember'.

So, you bring something that's solid and something that's easy to recall, and then what happens in the brain is that those memory patterns are attached to that thing.

Why that works is this...

We normally, mostly, use a system that I can call the P-I-D-S system, which is 'put it down somewhere.' So your head becomes a messy desk. Then, when you come to recall something, you find that your subconscious mind, and whichever bit of the brain it's using trying to recall those things, has to check a lot of connections.

It has to look round, which drawer was this bit in, what empty coffee cup did I put that in, has the scribbled note under the keyboard got anything to do with this. That's hard work as you have to make all the connections.

The thing is, if you have a *specific centre*, something that *you've imagined* in your head that's *easy to find*, you become the most fun filing system you can imagine.

Memory is only a connection of synapses in the brain anyway, the model. So if we've got one that we've already put all the connections in, we are much more likely to remember the substance of what we're trying to recall, usually without any effort at all.

Jane: And how do we add emotion to that?

Jon: Turn it into a game.

And you can apply that to anything. Make it a game.

If it's a game it's enjoyable, and play.

Now obviously this isn't the only way to remember, anyone who says there is only one way and that's their way, lives in a cave, or rather they should do.

Another very quick way of remembering stuff, and making it a game is covered in the next strategy, that of repetition.

I do this on stage in a demonstration. It's quite fun. I get somebody up on the stage and I say, what's your name?

And they'll say, Jane.

So I'll say, okay, Jane. Jane. What we're going to do here, Jane, is we're going to demonstrate to the audience, Jane. Yeah? Jane. Jane, Jane, Jane, Jane.

We're going to demonstrate to the audience, Jane; how to remember a name.

Jane.

Name.

Jane... Jane Mansfield...

There you go.

That's nice, isn't it?

Oh, that's a lovely smile. Name Jane.

You look like ... you look like ... oh, I know a Jane.

There was a girl at school called Jane Savage.

You look just like her.

Yes? Okay.

Now what happens then in the demonstration, I turn around and I ask the audience what your name is and everybody knows your name. Why?

Because I've said it seven or eight times. I've repeated it over and over and over.

I've also added a container that's easy for my subconscious to find, one that just popped into my head, and created a mnemonic.

And that's another easy way of developing a massively good memory is repeat stuff to yourself.

How do you think actors learn their lines?

They repeat them over and over and over again. When you were at school, most of the stuff you remember in the classes at school were the parrot-fashion repetitions.

Jane: Like the times table.

Jon: Like the times tables, which only lasts on average for a few years at school where we need it.

Jane: The seven times table. Nobody remembers the seven times table. I don't know why, but yes. Six sevens are ... yes, precisely.

Jon: 42. But I hated it and doubled the 3 times seven I do remember.

         But back to the remembering names game. Now the thing is, while you're doing this, and this is a subconscious skill ... while you're doing this, guess what's happening?

         The person's noticing consciously that you're doing it.

Jane: And I bet they're saying, why are you doing that?

Jon: And you say, "Because if I repeat your name seven times I'll remember it. My name's Jon. What's my name?"

And they go, "Jon." usually they're beginning to smile now because Mostly their subconscious enjoys games too.

So I say, "what's my name?" again…

They say, "Jon."

I then say, "See? You're beginning to remember it now. Who do you know is famous with the name Jon?"

"John Wayne." Is one I've heard a lot along with Travolta, which says a lot about the people I speak for and train!

Now I'm increasing the repetition and adding a mnemonic for them, because I want them to remember me.

"Well, okay. Have a look at me. Now I'm John Wayne. What do you see?"

"Well, I see a hat and a gun, and…"
That's their mnemonic.

That's a way of very, very quickly developing your memory for names and making sure they remember yours while you bring a bit of value to their lives.

And you can apply that to anything. Make it a game.

Now the thing is, if you feel a little bit embarrassed because people have noticed and everything, embarrassment is a subconscious emotion.

And you can actually use that embarrassment to make it a game and to make it an experiment.

And that brings about the production of dopamine and the other neurotransmitters which means you, and the person you're playing with, both create the Mental Modelling we call memory a lot faster - it's a miracle!

Doing It Again

Jane: Doing it again. Now having worked with you for over 18 years this is obvious to me. Although we've refined trainings, modernised them and their delivery and language, basically it's still the same message, methods and results. Can we clarify for the reader just what we mean by "Doing it again."

Jon: Yes. That's it.

Jane and Jon (Laugh)

Jon: Doing it again simply means **repetition**.

         In the last chapter we talked about memory creation using repetition.

         It's a skill that we have from birth.

         It's a skill that we've been using a lot for most of our life.

         We're having a conversation now using a language we both learnt through repetition.

What happened was, you were making baby noises, and somebody said your name, Jane. You heard it, and you repeated it, "Jane," and they said, "Jane." "Jane." "Jane." "Jane." "Jane." "Jane." To the point where you knew that that was your name.

Most Babies first word is something like Momma, or Daddy, because that's what parents with a touch of narcissism say to their kids over and over.

Repetition is built in subconsciously like our talents and traits. My youngest son James's first word was "Bugger"… and that got me into loads of trouble when his Mum stopped laughing!

We learned to speak by repetition.

We learned to walk by repetition.

We learned to talk by repetition.

We learned to drive by repetition.

We learned to write by repetition.

We learned to type by repetition.

We learn everything that we've learned by repetition.

We do it, and when it's successful, **we do it again.**

And the more we do something, the better we get at it, the more comfortable it becomes and the more confident we become at doing it.

Now, one of the problems with professional communication is that people forget that.

A few years ago I was on a speaking course. I've done lots of speaking courses, I'm a learning junkie and love to be a student as much as a teacher.

Some of the courses I've done have been magic, some of them have been tragic and no, I'm not mentioning any names.

I was on one course, and one of the people that I was in a small practise group with said, "I've got to have three talks."

I said, "Why?"

He said, "I've got three audiences. I've got three niches I'm targeting, so I've got to have three talks."

Now this was a feed-back practice so I said, "No, you don't. You just need to have the same talk for each niche."

He said, "Oh, that's ridiculous."

Now I've been in show business for 30 years with the same act.

I don't change my act.

I change the way I *present* that act, but I don't change my act.

I don't change my talk. I don't change my speech, because I'm very good at that, and I know that it works.

When I figured out what works, I do it again. If the audience laugh, I do it again. If the audience don't laugh, I don't do that again.

I do something else until the audience laugh, and then I do it again, but then I do it again, and do it again, and do it again, and do it again, and that has two effects.

Number one, I remember it. Number two, I get very, very good at it.

Now, when you think of, let's take Britain's most popular soap, 'EastEnders', which I do have to go on record as saying I do not watch, but I used to for about two years.

Now, I can guarantee that every Christmas Day, there is an horrendously traumatic, horrible thing that happens on EastEnders every single Christmas.

Why? Because when something terrible happens at a point in time where most people are off and watching the damn thing, they put in a hugely dramatic event because their viewing figures go up.

Why do they do it again, and why do they do it again, and why do they do it again, and why do all soaps, why do comedies, why do films, why does everything follow a set format?

Why do they do it again, and do it again, and do it again?

Because as human beings, we are inclined to do it again, and do it again, and do it again.

We're very habitual creatures. We're very ritualistic creatures. It's part of our whole society. It's part of our whole makeup.

We invented religion for exactly the do it again thing, so that you can go into your church, your temple, your synagogue, your mosque or whatever it is, and you can do it again, and again, and again, and again. It makes you feel good. It makes you feel like you belong. It makes you feel comfortable…

Go to a football match and watch a football crowd like the one at Molinuex Ground, home of the Wolves, Wolverhampton Wanderers, they are very, very good at chanting and singing. (That's my team, by the way.)

They'll go into a chant, and they repeat it over, and over, and over, and over, and over again, but you can go into a village in the centre of Africa that have never seen a football match, and you listen to what they do.

They have likewise very ritualistic tribal events, and they'll be repeating the song, the dance, the ritual. And do it again, and do it again, and do it again, and do it again.

This is nature. Nature does that all the time. If it works, do it again. If it works, do it again. If it works, do it again.

Now, hopefully, we're getting through that if your subconscious mind does something that's great and fabulous, do it again. If your subconscious mind does something that isn't, tell it it's wrong.

Tell it off. Treat it like a child. Tell it no then tell it why.

As I explained with the Peter Paul story, it's when Paul is really getting up Peter's nose, Peter should turn around and say, "Look, Paul. I don't think this is a good idea, So, let's not do that again, what if we do this instead…"

I know there is the idea that if at first you don't succeed, try try try again until it does work, but do you know that takes an awful lot of time, and a lot of the time you then have to join the idea of there being no such thing as failure and you end up learning that the bloody thing doesn't work so go do something else anyway.

It's much easier to find the stuff that does work and do that again.

Jane: What you're saying is, if someone gets
        stuck but they keep repeating it and never
        getting good at it, then they should stop?

Jon: Probably. If you think that didn't work,
        don't do it. If you think, "Well, that
        worked magnificently well." Do it again.

        Don't be scared of repeating a rewarding
        action. It doesn't mean you're an
        obsessive compulsive. Habits and rituals
        are fine if they help you get success.

'The Rapid Repetition Routine'

Jon   Here's what has been called power self-
        suggestion.

        There's a game most, if not all, kids do as
        they are learning language and we like
        games don't we.

        Take the Couéism, 'Every day in every
        way I'm getting better and better'.

        Shorten that down to a single word, in
        this case 'better' is probably the best
        keyword.

Say '*better*' out loud to yourself and *repeat it so fast and so often it stops making conscious sense* and then continue to say it.

You'll sound, and maybe feel, a little demented doing this so pick somewhere to do it where you won't get arrested in, or thrown out of.

If that's not possible put on a look of distracted otherworldliness, shove in a couple of earphone buds and, 'sing' it under your breath. Who'll know?

Do this for a minute.

This works to get the thing into your imaginative mind like a steam train.....

Repeating your keyword rapidly until the same thing happens that happens when kids are using repetition to subconsciously learn.

Keep doing it until the *conscious logical brain stops listening* and doing the work.

Do it until the logic runs out and until the *word* just becomes the *sounds* you're making.

Once the *word stops making sense* to your intellectual brain it gives up and gives control to your subconscious.

Once your Mind, your subconscious is saying your keyword then it's just like self suggestions - automatic, without thought, and likewise extremely effective.

It will even get to the point where just thinking about your keyword will run the whole routine automatically.

Then you really are firing on all cylinders.

The Simplify Skill

Jane: I know you'd list one of your greatest skills as that of being able to always see the simplest way to do things. We'll talk about the 'always' later, but, what's the simplification skill? And how do we do that?

Jon: Einstein is attributed … We've got to be very careful with quotes nowadays. Einstein is **attributed** with saying, "Everything should be made as simple as possible but not simpler." My favourite quote.

I'm intrinsically lazy and always on the look out for the fastest, easiest and ultimately the most fun way of doing everything.

Now obviously the esteemed Albert E, was renowned for coming up with really massive, huge, great big mile-long equations that made things simple if you understood the equations.

He still managed to encapsulate them in ever decreasing equations until he came up with $E=Mc^2$ to basically explain that everything is energy - even mass.

But if you think of your subconscious mind as a bright nine-year-old, and we talked about that in Meet Your Subconscious, if you think of that subconscious mind as a bright nine-year-old and you think, well, I have to simplify this concept for my subconscious mind to get it on board and to understand it. I have to simplify it into the terms that I would use to explain it to a nine-year-old child.

Then more often or not you'll find the easiest and most effective way to go.

That's what I did with SubSkills, it's not about making what I'm doing more complex. It's not about learning more skills. It's about learning to use the skills that we've got on board.

It's all about simplifying our strategies.

It's rather like baking bread. There is a simple strategy for baking bread.

Once you've done it a few times and you're following the recipe, then you can bake a fairly successful loaf pretty much every single time. Because you've simplified it to the point where it's just as few steps as possible.

I love watching people who've found the way in what they are doing. The expert who's doing the job and who can watch you and say, 'do you know, there's a simpler easier way of doing that. Why don't you just put that over there, and that works?'

That's where I come from, as an Observer Mind STYLE it's how I'm wired. I come from that point of, let's make it as simple, as easy as possible. Because the simpler it is, the faster it is, the more productive it is, and the more certain we are of getting the same result.

So, it's about looking at everything that we do and everything that we're learning and thinking, and asking the question, is that complex? Does it need to be that complicated? Do we need that much detail? Do we need to get into that much complexity and that much understanding?

Obviously, well, some people do need ALL of the detail. Some people need the detail and some people need the understanding and some people need to do loads of research.

That doesn't mean that when you come to do the thing that you've been learning and the thing that you've been researching, like subconscious skills, that we have to make it complex.

There's an old marketing term, K-I-S-S. that stands for: 'Keep it simple, stupid'. Don't get into too much detail if you don't have to.

Don't get into too many routines where you've got one crossing over the other and you've got to think about this and then think about that and then think about that.

Because you're just going to go into overload mode, and when you go into overload mode things will start to break down very, very quickly. Especially in a conversation, especially in communication. Especially subconsciously. So the simpler you can make it, the better.

One of the easiest tricks I find to do things simply is to *break them down into little bits*. What used to be called ... and I forget where it came from; I think it might have been NLP, but I'm not sure ... and that is chunking.

That is taking any task and breaking it down into steps and *focusing* on each step *one at a time*.

So think of whatever it is you want to do, *think of it in little stages* and do each little bit at a time. Oprah says, "don't get overcome by complexity, you know, just do the next right thing".

And it's very much a case of that. It's very much a case of, do the next thing first and don't worry about the other ones, just *do the next thing first.*

And when you've completed the next thing, you move on to the next step, or stage or strategy.

Simplify by cutting everything, every task, every conversation, every venture, every adventure, every relationship, everything, cut them down into the little bits that we need to do.

Piece by piece by piece. And always simplify it. Always simplify it.

Never allow the complexity to overcome and overwhelm you.

Seductive Self Suggestions

Jane: Seductive suggestions sounds like an interesting skill.

Jon: Obviously, being a hypnotist for many, many years, people have asked me to explain to them, suggestions.

A common question is, "What is a suggestion, Jon?" Is that me saying, "I think it'd be a great idea if the window was open, because it'd be cooler in here?"

And I have to answer no, that's not really a suggestion in the terms that we're using, in the terms that we're saying seductive self-suggestion think more of a desirable psychological suggestion.

For example maybe I'd say, "You know oxygen makes your mind work better… so does being cooler. The windows need to be opened." Then I'd look at the person I want to open the window and wait. Usually, they will smile, or sigh, get up and open a window. That works 80% of the time, which is acceptably good.

They feel like it was their idea which of course it wasn't, and they'll forget what happened almost immediately.

I could say, "Opening a window would make it cooler in here." That's an idea or a plan put forward for consideration and that's what the dictionary terminology says about suggestion.

Synonyms for suggestion in the dictionary are proposal, preposition, motion, submission, action point, recommendation, advice, counsel, but none of those things really hit what we're talking about here in Subconscious Skills. That's why I've added the word seductive - *tempting and attractive.*

In the window suggestion above we **start with what sounds like a fact**. That oxygen makes the brain work better... that is *actually* the suggestion. Everyone wants a better working brain - well mostly. Likewise most people don't want to be seen as having a brain that isn't working well.

The idea we're implanting is to get the brain working better - *desirable*.

That is followed by supplying a **simple solution** which we know the subconscious mind will do because it's easier to f*ollow a response supplied* than to figure it out yourself.

So we Make it *tempting*. Make it *attractive, enticing*, using a seductive, almost provocative result.

If you're doing a video promotion for a book, rather than saying, 'Here. Here's my book,' hold the book. Caress the book and say, 'I'd like to give you a copy of my book. Would you like me to sign it?' If you say that in a tone that *suggests, implants the feeling, that there's something special about this*, that there's something *intimate* about this...

Jane: ...implying that there's something special about the person, because you're saying that you're going to sign it?

Jon: Yes 'I would **love** to sign this for **you**.'
Notice the language there. I'm not doing
it for me. I'm doing it for you. That's
alluring. That's enticing. It's tempting, isn't
it? Much more tempting than, 'Here's my
card.'

Jane: So, it makes you more influential in the
sense that you are making *them feel more
important* because you're giving them an
idea of their importance to you. And
because you're using particular language
which they're not particularly aware of, it's
causing more intimacy between you?

Jon: Yes You've been listening haven't you.

And you know I don't have to be aware
of it, either. I don't have to consciously
think about this. I just have to *tell* myself,
'I really do think that this is sexy, giving
you a book.' and let my subconscious do
all the rest…. It's good at it!

Choose Your Moods

Jane: Now, we hear a lot about mindsets these days? I remember it used to be that Attitude was the buzz term and of course positive thinking is still holding on. And I know that you prefer to simplify this down to a simple concept Jon, that of moods. So, tell us about moods and why they are so important.

Jon: 50% of your personality is pretty much written into your DNA, it's hardwired. It doesn't change.

It's the part that governs your most likely behavioural traits, tendencies and talents.

That's why people who have a certain character when they're an infant, before they've learnt their place in society or anything like that and before they've been influenced by society, still pretty much have the same base character when they grow up, and on the day they die. Their character is pretty much the same.

We cover that more in the MindStyleapp and book. I do not believe, as some people seem to think, your mindSET.

According to most psychology research Mindset is a theory. One that the self help and therapy movement evangelists love to wave around at exactly the same time as they they tell us the brain is made of plasticine and can be made into Wallace or Gromit whenever we want. Which makes me wonder where the idea of 'set' comes from.

It looks most probable that our hard wired responses, coupled with the social acceptable ideas of where we fit, or in the case of a therapeutic approach where we don't fit, in the society we live in can be seen as a set of responses over which we have no control, or on the other hand we have absolute control.

I've said it before that personal and professional development is getting to look more like a religion, and as such there's a lot of purely taken on faith rhetoric and theory out there.

A lot's said about mindset as if that's the holy grail of personal development, that if you've got this mindset, you can achieve everything. It's going to last, and last, and never, never ever, change unless of course you want it to. Then a bit of good old regressive therapy or cognitive behavioural intervention and bosh, new mindset which will never ever, ever change - except when it does...

Truth is that a mindset, which actually is 50% set and unchangeable, is 50% the mood that you're in, the chemical balance you're experiencing, and moods are very temporary. They're very transitory and change in a moment.

Nobody is angry forever. Anger may have different levels, and yes, you might get somebody who's pretty chuffed off most of the time, but nobody's angry 24 hours a day, 365 days of the year.

Nobody is anxious or sad that long. I know it can seem that way but when you look at it unless actually physically incapable of producing the right chemical balance in the brain, and we're not addressing actually ill, sick or broken people here.

Our moods *change*, and our moods change pretty swiftly, and they might only last for a while. And, by using the *natural events and triggers* that change our moods we can *choose* them at will.

I was mentoring a client up for an Executive position they'd been after for quite a while, and they said, 'I'm very anxious when I go into interview situations. What do I do about that?'

I said, "Well, choose a better mood." They said, "Well, how do I do that?"

What we decided to do with that person was, there was a *particular song* that put them in a *great mood* and made them feel 'Centred, and grounded and as confident as when I was six with my Grandma.'

I'm sorry, I forget the name of the song, but it did it for them.

It put them in such a great mood, but, it didn't last and the effect wore off in about an hour or so.

So I asked 'Right. On average, for the work you're going for, how long do the interviews last?'

They said, 'No longer than 45 minutes.'

I said, 'Right. Okay. If you listen to this song and you *keep repeating* the little bits that *stick in your head* every now and again like when you can, and you start repeating back the things that people are saying to you so that they can see that what they're saying is important …

They got the job with a significant preferable change in their lifestyle.

And you can *fine-tune that with practice and repetition*. Play and experiment with it at times when it doesn't matter so much.

It won't be long before you're doing it in the *mood that the song puts you into*, it should be the very last thing you do, the very last

thing you do for a couple of minutes
before you go into that interview, that
negotiation, that meeting, that...

Jane: Listen to the song?

Jon: **Listen to the song.** We all have what I
call *mood modifiers*. If you keep on board
your mood modifiers, then you can
choose the mood you want to have in
almost any situation.

Of course - unfortunately - there are
chemical mood modifiers like cigarettes,
alcohol, drugs. They're mood modifiers.
They change our feelings. They change
our temporary state.

The problem is, of course, nobody stays
in that state, so nobody gets a high where
they feel really, really good and giggly and
want some crisps, and stays there forever.
So they have to go down the road of
doing whatever it was that caused that,
and of course, we're not suggesting that
anybody should do anything illegal,
immoral or chemically addictive, because

you don't *need* to use those to modify your mood.

People forget to do this in situations where maybe they were going to be stressed. Maybe they were going to feel on edge. Obviously just being in a better mood would be more productive for them.

Now, you know I do not do positive and negative. I'll talk a little bit more about that, I think, later on, but I don't do positive or negative.

I do *productive* and *unproductive,* so if you have moods that you want to apply that make you more productive for an hour or so, then do whatever it takes before you go into the situation when you need that mood for the next hour or so, or if it's a mood that you've got to be in all day, then figure out a way of applying your *mood moderator* to produce that mood at regular intervals.

Now, the thing is, obviously, we've mentioned mood moderators that are not appropriate to be used constantly, consistently all the time. In fact, most of them should never be used, but people do. However, one of the things we can do to help our subconscious wellness and to help our subconscious success is to *choose the mood* that we need to be in, be that calm, excited, generous, careful whatever, in the situation that we're going into.

Then use our **mood modifier**.

Now it isn't always practical or possible to be around a video player or music producer or book or a dozen photos of your kids kids.

Actually you can do all those with a watch but, there are moments it's not doable. Maybe your batteries screw up or run down miles away from the nearest socket or charging block.

In the case of such natural disasters we can create mood modifiers through a thing we call *anchoring*, and anchoring can be used in conversation situations to get people to fire a mood that's better for them as well, that requires a much longer explanation. Basically anchoring is just attaching a *physical* or *mental* action that runs the same response as any of our mood moderators. Using anchors we can attach something we do that no one else really notices to an event or thing that gets us in the right mood.

One thing that I've told many, many executives and business owners who use the telephone a lot is to make sure that they anchor a mood modifier to their telephone.

Of course with the smart phone we can just use a photo as a backdrop but say some idiot has dared to call your land line.

Anchor a mood moderator to the action of *picking up a handset and putting it to your ear.* You do that simply by looking at the picture, playing the music, smelling the roses - whatever - and then you act out picking up the handset and talking.

Obviously you need to be feeling the productive feeling you want, even if it's only slight, and you need to *repeat* this often.

Jane: So I just keep doing it till it sticks?

Jon: **Until it becomes part of your response yes**. I know a lot of people who use anchoring tell you to apply an action such as touching a certain finger with your thumb, lifting an eyebrow, tilting your head or even making massive movements with your gestures but, I'm lazy so I just *use the action* I'm going to be doing anyway.

They all work of course, just with the others you have to remember which anchor fits, with this method it's easy to forget to remember once it's in your set.

Jane: So choose your moods.

Jon: Yes. Remember that you can choose them, and just use a mood moderator to change the mood for whichever mood you need to be in to achieve the most success to what you're going into, the conversation, the negotiation, or whatever.

Just another example. I do know one guy who's an extremely good negotiator. When he needs to go into a situation where he knows he's going to need to impress and be seen as the 'guru' figure, he reads or recites the 'We will fight them on the beaches' speech from Churchill.

When he thinks he's going to need to be on the back foot and a little more gentle and a little more praising, he uses the 'I Have a Dream' speech from Martin Luther King.

I'm not saying that either of those speeches, in you, would project exactly the same mood, but those are his mood moderators for those two situations when he's going into a negotiation.

So there, we've anchored something and all you've got to do is use that for a couple of seconds before you go in, and the thing's running then in your mind for an hour or so.

Moods tend to last for an hour or so.

Comfortable Excitement

Jane: Now, my favourite idea skill, that I've personally had a lot of success with and think you definitely need to have, is ***relaxed excitement in your comfort zone***. What do you mean by that?

Jon: Have you ever heard that doing nothing and going nowhere means you're stuck in your comfort zone?

Jane: Yes.

Jon: Right. Have you ever read a phrase like, "Everything that's good, especially all growth, happens the other side of your comfort zone"?

Jane: Yes.

Jon: They are both bollocks, or gonads for our Non-Brit friends.

Your comfort zone is your natural GPS that tells you that you are exactly where you **should** be doing the things you **should** be doing.

The idea that people who are lethargic are comfortable, or that stress and fear are productive is a massive misnomer. I'm not a 'therapist' but in mind coaching several thousand people, one thing is obvious; people who are not where they should be are **not** comfortable. And in my observations everyone I've interviewed, mentored, talked to who are *really successful experts* are naturally comfortable with who they are and what they do.

Let's take a quick look at where the idea of better stuff happening when you're uncomfortable, comes from.

Many years ago, many, many years ago, in the 1920s, two animal behavioralists called Yerkes and Dodson did a little experiment called the "dancing mouse" experiment. Robert M. Yerkes and John D. Dodson (1908)

First published in Journal of Comparative Neurology and Psychology,.18, 459-482.

Basically they were testing how quickly mice would stay out of a compartment in a nesting block if they gave it a shock of electricity every time it went in.

The result of course was that a mouse, called a 'dancer' presumably because of the jumping it did to avoid an electrified floor, learnt to avoid the electrified compartment faster under stress.

It didn't take a massive leap from there for the burgeoning new science of psychology to apply the same theory to humans.

Yerkes wrote "*Anxiety improves performance until a certain optimum level of arousal has been reached. Beyond that point, performance deteriorates as higher levels of anxiety are attained.*"

A LOT of behavioural science is based on the poor rodents of this world, rats and mice being particular favourites, apparently they share a lot of neurological makeup, that's why you see loads of them at university lectures and networking meetings.

Nothing happened about that for years and years and years, and then it was mentioned in a book in the 1960s when the term *comfort zone* was put directly at American corporate institutions, that they were in this comfort zone where nothing was happening. They were comfortable, and there were no changes, and there was no progression being made, and that sort of thing.

Now, in the religion of personal development, and it is a religion. It is a religion. It's got priests. It's got evangelists. It's got agnostics like me. The agnostics tend to sit on the fence and say, 'Well, maybe that's not true, although it could be...' but in the religion of personal development, it's become a mantra now that if you're in your 'comfort zone', it means you're not doing anything. It means you're stuck, stymied, stale. You're not doing anything.

Do you know, every single person I've ever mentored is in some way stuck, stymied, stale? Every company that I've ever worked with is stuck, stymied, stale.

None of those have been comfortable.
They've all been **uncomfortable,** and
that's why they want to move on, because
they're not comfortable with where they
are. They may well be in a Lethargy Zone,
but it's not comfortable.

At the other end of the scale you have
people shouting - and they do tend to be
the more shouty style of evangelists, they
yell; 'You have to take massive action.
You have to *push* yourself forward. You
have to *take risks.*'

A lot of them have been saying that self
same mantra for decades bless them,
because they're comfortable doing that
and saying it, because they're comfortable
repeating those things.

Remember what we said about do it
again? We're very habitual creatures,
human beings.

There's nothing wrong with that, by the
way. It's absolutely fabulous, because if
we weren't habitual, you'd forget to brush

your teeth and watch your favourite shows.

Facebook absolutely relies on it. However in the comfort zone, and it really is a misnomer, the assumption that if you're under a lot of stress and pressure, you're more effective.

No, you're not. No, you're not.

When I've challenged that assumption, based on a dancing mouse remember, I often get the reply 'Oh, well, yeah, but you're more productive when you're doing stuff in the optimal stress zone just outside of being comfortable. doing new stuff.'

And I agree. Yes, you are doing stuff, and yes, I mean, there are so many great leaders in the entrepreneurial world, the entrepreneurial priests and evangelists, who suggest we've got to move forward. We've got to do this, and we've got to do that, and we've got to be uncomfortable before we can get comfortable again. And then we've got to go and do it all again…

I'll admit there are people wired that way, in the MindSTYLEapp we call them Performers. And that's *their* comfort zone, being on the edge.

But it isn't meant for everyone. I see a lot of people trying to attain success that way, even succeeding sometimes but...

Sadly, a lot of those die prematurely in their 50s with few or no friends because they've been under stress and pressure for so long. Even though they, look like they're enjoying it, the body simply can't take it.

We are designed to be comfortable not stressed. We are not designed to be lethargic but we are designed to avoid danger, be that a sabre toothed tiger or the IRS. And anyone who tells you that the good old flight or fight response is redundant in this wonderful modern world, well they need to get out more frankly.

Now, here is my version of the much hated Venn diagram giving an idea of where the comfort zone is.

You can go from one side of that comfort zone to almost doing nothing, to the other side of the comfort zone where you're almost in stress. Anywhere outside of that *isn't* productive one way or the other.

To the left of the comfort zone as we look at it, is the mood that we call excitement, where you're not scared and anxious, but you are where your heart is pumping. You do have noradrenaline. You do have lots of dopamine. You do have lots of feel-good endorphins in your body, but you're not actually scared not really anxious. You're not frightened. You're excited.

It's a bit like going on a rollercoaster ride or jumping out of an aeroplane with a knapsack on your back and a bit of cloth in it with some string tied to it and going, "Whee," as you drop like a stone towards the earth.

Now, people who do that are not really in the stress zone. They're in the excitement edge of their comfort zone.

Jane: And that's what you mean by relaxed excitement.

Jon: Yes. What I mean by relaxed excitement in the comfort zone is that you're on a rollercoaster ride. You're on a ride. You're excited, but you know there's really no danger, or very little danger.

           If you went onto a rollercoaster ride, and I know accidents do happen, accidents happen everywhere to everything, but if there was more than 1%, and it's probably less than that, chance of you being injured or killed, you wouldn't go on the ride, would you?

That would be stupid, but you go on the ride because it gives you the feeling that it might be a bit dangerous, and it might be a bit scary. But you don't go into stress mode.

Most people can handle that, but you can be on the rollercoaster ride. You can be excited. Your heart can beat, but there's that strange feeling of still feeling comfortable. You know you're excited not terrified.

Do you know what I mean? Still being relaxed where your breathing's high, but it's not way past the score. Your heart rate's high, but it's not terminally high. Your adrenalin's high, but you're not really going to run away. You can override it and that's excitement.

Jane: So it's like looking forward to something? You know, really looking forward to something exciting that you're going to be doing or that you're doing.

Jon: Yes.

Jane: So what you're saying is that people who
         are being told to get out of their comfort
         zones because they're lethargic, they're
         not going anywhere, they're doing things
         habitually and they're not growing.

         And by saying to these people, "You've
         got to get out of that, step outside of
         your comfort zone." What you're saying is
         that actually that's their discomfort zone
         and to move into their comfort zone
         where they're excited and happy.

Jon: Well. It's their *discomfort* zone if they don't
         want to be there.

         Not everyone has to be striving all the
         time. I've met loads of perfectly happy
         and content people and comfortable
         people who in a small way contribute to
         the experience and to our lifestyle.

         I'll guess they won't be reading this book.
         they are happy. Good for them.

So we've got discomfort, we've got stress, and in the middle we've got comfort and we can go everywhere in the comfort zone from being totally chilled and laid out and doing nothing and vegging, but not stuck there. Watching Netflix or if you're like me, you know, Amazon Prime.

But sitting there and doing nothing for a few hours and just turning your brain off from watching the telly and having a great time. Or you can be doing something that's getting the adrenalin going, something that's exciting you, something that's making you feel excited.

There's a lot of research been done on this. Prof Ian Robertson of Trinity College Dublin. His latest book, *'The Stress Test'* talks about how simply changing the idea of being anxious or scared with the mood of being excited, can alter cortisol levels in the brain and reduce the 'stress' chemical toxic effects.

In a Northumbrian college, a group of students who all reported that they were scared of their exams were studied. 50%

of them they did nothing with them, the other 50%, they got them in and they said, "Instead of feeling fear, tell yourself you're excited. Tell yourself you're excited. Tell yourself you're excited. I'm not scared, I'm excited."

Now what that did in their subconscious was to *change the chemical composition* in their brain. So that they went into the same situation with the same physiology, but *slightly different emotions* and therefore, *slightly different responses*. And therefore, slightly different *mood* and therefore, slightly different *reactions* and yes, they changed their mood and all of them did better than the control group.

They were still physiologically the same ... Their hearts were racing, but they were excited about doing the competition instead of fearing it.

Jane: Competition?

Jon: Well let's face it, that's the way we see a test. That's the way we see an exam. It's competition, it's us against whoever set the exam, or our rival students, or just against ourselves and our expectations.

And you go into that competition and a lot of people compete. I've worked with sports people and they compete, even show biz people… A lot of people are in a competition situation. And if you go into the competition situation in an *excited mode,* rather than a *scared mode*, you will relax mentally and reduce the toxic problems people get with stress. So you get an excited relaxation or a *relaxed excitement*, because you're *in* **your comfort zone**. You're feeling comfortable about that. And of course if you're feeling comfortable, you're feeling confident.

So the results of the 50% who changed the way they felt about the exam were better than those still nervous and anxious.

Jane: Wow can't wait to try that one!

Jon: Just a bit of advice. If you really can't think "I'm just excited." Don't do it until you can.

143

So learning and developing these subskills should be exciting, and enjoyable. It should *never* be stressful.

If you're facing the fear and going through it anyway, then the wrong chemistry is happening inside you and you don't want that to happen. *Excitement* is good. *Fear* is bad.

Don't do fear, there's no reason to. And I will also tell people, 'Well if you're really, really scared, don't do it. Because even if you learn to do it, you're never going to be as good as you could have been, had you been doing something that didn't scare you and you will burn out faster.'

You know, the body just can't take that chemistry all the time. So a mistake is an action or judgement that's sort of like misguided or it's wrong.

So making it too complex, trying to do too much. You know, an expert is somebody who knows the simplest, easiest way of doing that and they do it over and over and over again.

Envoi: I'm not saying we can't handle stress and anxiety.

We can certainly change phobias and unproductive fears to excitement.

And yes we can and do face our **discomfort** and do it anyway, but if whatever we were scared of still causes us to feel uncomfortable, or if what we were scared of is still dangerous or unproductive, then we probably won't do it anyway, or we can burn out and suffer injury through hidden stress.

For clarity we're not talking unreasonable overactive terror, that's a phobia and that is a condition that needs treatment. Then our subconscious needs to be taught a different response.

Mistakes, Myths, and Misunderstandings to avoid

Making It Complicated

Jane: What's the number one mistake we make, when using our subconscious skills?

Jon: Well I think the number one mistake really is to make it too complicated. Make everything too complex, trying to do too much. Trying to do so much we start to do something human brains are useless at and that's multi-tasking.

Subconsciously we need the simple life.

Of course, as with any skillset, as we develop you have to go through a conscious state first with reading or listening. Making a competition out of your life enterprise adds complexity too.

If you're making it a win or a lose situation, instead of a let's see what the result's going to be situation. If you're doing those things and then you add something to something else, then you're over complicating it. You're making it too complex.

I see this time and time again, where people have learned a very, very good technique, a very good method, honed and tested and refined by experience and observation. And then they change it.

They add another technique that they think might work.

They add braces, that's suspenders, to a belt.

Don't do that until you've at least tried both of them individually. Because, you might not need both. Does that make sense?

Jane: Yes. So you're basically saying that you
         need to use something that works simply
         in the first place?

Jon: Yes. And if that's not working for you,
         stop and do something else.

Jane: Yes.

Jon: Don't try and add something else to what
         you're doing.

Jane: So if you try the braces and they don't
         work for you, then take them off and try
         a belt. Yes?

Jon: Yes, but sit down before you put the belt
         on, because if you take the braces off and
         they're not working, then your trousers
         could fall to the floor and that could be
         embarrassing. Next one please?

You Don't Have To Change

Jane: I've heard you say often that the saying
         'you have to change' is a myth. Is that the
         biggest myth that frustrates you that's still
         around with subconscious skills?

149

Jon: I think the number one myth is you have to change, yes.

If you're not getting the results you want in whatever it is you're doing, YOU don't have to change.

You don't have to become somebody you're not, nor should you have to become like somebody else...

You know, I've seen the high priests of personal development say this, that you should never take anybody's opinion of who you are and what you are on board.

I agree but I still see people being told they should follow the behaviours of their guru.

And there's a little bit of humbug there that very few people have noticed, but it's there all the time. That you have to change, you have to become somebody, something different to who you are and what you know. And that's entirely untrue. What you do have to do, I believe, is become more you.

Don't become a brand or a poor copy of the master. Be yourself and become present.

Now there has been a move over the last five or six years, which has been really brilliant, where people are getting more and more Authentic.

Now you know me, if we go into a social situation. I go in with my magic wallet, which is a wallet that's absolutely full of mentalist effects and props, and all sorts of things. And I will generally find myself a corner, well okay the middle of the room… and I will gather a few people around me and I start doing mind-reading and stuff like that, because that's what I enjoy doing in social situations.

I like doing that at conferences at lunchtime and sometimes in the after show bar. But that's me, not trying to be Derren Brown. **It's very much a mistake that you have to be somebody else, you have to change.**

You don't.

You have to be the best you, the best version of you. Not like somebody else.

One of the worst things you can do is try to totally emulate somebody else, because when you try to emulate somebody else, all you can ever be is a bad copy of that person.

Jane: Yes I agree with that.

Jon: Now I know the modelling doctrine says that if you do what the expert does, you become the expert. If you do what that person's doing, you become that person.

Very likely you do, but it's very, very, very rare to find people able to model the outliers and it's the outliers that you hear about.

It's the people who do the million in five months, it's the people who appear on the stages that you've been dreaming about for 20 years and they seem to have come from nowhere got on those stages. It's those people that you hear about.

Because they're the big successes and they are absolutely in the minority.

But almost always when you look at that person, you look at the guru that they had, you look at the mentor that they had, you'll see that there's vast differences. They seem to be doing the same thing, but they're not. They're doing it very individually. And when you look at gurus, they'll say, "Do what I do and become me."

I never say that to people I mentor. I say, "Here's a strategy you can use," but it's *all about you* and *it's all about getting to know your subconscious mind*, getting to know what your subconscious mind wants. Getting to know who your subconscious mind is and then being the person that lives with that subconscious mind, to the point where you're working together. Instead of saying, 'Am I there yet?'

The secret is, it's about being you, not changing who you are.

The Subconscious is Unreasonable and Programmable

Jane: And what about the biggest misunderstanding you see around subconscious success people often have, where they think in their minds that they're actually doing the right thing and don't realise it's a misunderstanding?

Jon: I think misunderstanding might be the wrong word, because then that's a failure to understand something correctly. I think that the idea of the subconscious process .... some people call it non-conscious, some people call unconscious, some people call it autonomic; but we're going to use subconscious.

It's your emotive process and I think that it's a misunderstanding that it is somehow a computer. A computer is a handy analogy to use, just as you could use a robot to describe your body, but I promise you, having been in a position where I've been able to see inside of a few human bodies, that they don't look like computers or technology when you get in there.

You know, hearts are different sizes, organs are different sizes, veins and arteries are in slightly different places. You know, it's not like an Apple store in there, where you know what's going on inside and things are different.

We know that simple little things like the shape and the size of the pituitary gland can make the difference between a manic depressive and not. You know, a physiological thing can make a difference. And I think it's a misunderstanding that this subconscious process is programmable in the same way as a computer is programmed.

I think most of us are to a degree hard wired subconsciously, as we know through mind style. That much of our subconscious is hard wired, but even then it's not hard wired to be precisely one thing or another.

There's different definitions of how that can work out. And I think it's also the idea, that you see very often written down, is that the subconscious mind is just an idiot. It just does the same thing over and over and over again. It never reasons, should I do something different or why do I want to do this?

I believe it does and in the experiments that I've conducted ... Being a stage hypnotist led me to the point where I could conduct experiments with the subconscious mind, that a therapist or psychologist would never dare to go near.

You know, because I can do that being on the edge, because people were on stage and they were working in every sort of situation from army bases to factories. All sorts of situations, where you've got all sorts of age ranges and all sorts of demographic people.

And in my observations, I think the subconscious mind can be influenced. I think the subconscious mind can be seduced if you like, but it doesn't stay like that because you can post a hypnotic suggestion into people, but it wears off. And sometimes it takes years and years and years to wear off, but sometimes it doesn't.

Although, direct suggestion does work, but how long that's going to work we don't know.

So I think it's a misunderstanding that A, the subconscious mind is programmable and B, that the subconscious mind is stupid. That it doesn't reason, it doesn't think things through, it only ever reacts, which is wrong.

It does think about things and it does have a problem solving process, just like the conscious has a problem solving process, but it does it from an internalised reality.

As we said, you know, what is the subconscious? It is an internalised reality and it comes at it with a different level of maturity, but it does reason. And I think it is a big misunderstanding to think that it's stupid, because if you think that, it'll come back and slap you.

Massive Motivation

Comfortable Confidence

Jane: Can you clarify a bit on what exactly is the advantage of being comfortably confident?

Jon: **Confidence** really is about being **comfortable with yourself**, more than anything else. I've never met an anxious, comfortable person, an actual confident person.

You can't be confidently anxious and you can't be anxiously confident.

I've seen confidence faked of course, a lot of strategists suggest we do this, I disagree. There's no need to fake it till you make it if you just make it first.

Confidence is; I am sure of this, I am happy with this, I'm relaxed with this, I'm comfortable with this.

And the more comfortable you get with who you are subconsciously, the more comfortable you get with the skills that you're using consciously, the more comfortable you become in a situation, the more comfortably confident you become.

And what that means is then, you naturally move on to the next thing, which of course is becoming more influential.

Because, we are led by and follow the people who are confident about what they're doing.

Our leaders are comfortable with being leaders. And I'm talking natural leaders.

The biggest influencers are comfortable with doing what they're doing.

Now I know you might get an actor saying, "Oh yeah, but I'm always nervous when I go out on stage."

For nervous read excited. You know, people think that nervous isn't desirable but exciting is. Well say to your subconscious, 'I get that you are excited but are you terrified?'

'If it answers, 'Well no, I'm not terrified, because if I was terrified then I wouldn't be here. I'm excited. I'm nervous about it, I'm thrilled about it, and I'm comfortable with that.' Then that's a good place to be for a while, that's confidence.

And that's working within your comfort zone. So *confidence* comes from *comfort* and comfort comes because you're confident about something.

Increased Influence

Jane: Increased influence that you just mentioned. What do we get most from increased influence?

Jon: More respect. More attention and more opportunities...

If you put your success down, as we said before, as being something that you repeat that gives you a reward and it's become easy to do. It's still a challenge because you don't know ... It's still an experiment. Instead of challenge, think experiment.

And it's still an experiment, but the better you become at who you are and what you do, then the more influential you become.

When you start telling people who you are and what you want, then you *attract* the people who want the same sort of result and reward.

Most likely you've got more skills on board that you can give them, more experience on board that you can give them, more knowledge on board that you can give them.

That above almost anything else brings value to peoples' lives and when you do that you're *influencing people*.

And we're talking influence, which is about who you are and what you do, not persuasion which is you trying to manipulate people to take what you want them to have without necessarily being it yourself.

When you influence people they will happily do some sort of exchange with you to get those skills and to be taught those things, or to get that service.

So, the benefit from increasing your influence is more people. More people are joining in with your **lifestyle enterprise**, whatever that is.

Personal Presence

Jane: And of course, personal presence is obviously something we all should want. Yes?

Jon: It's not something we should want, it's what most people who are professional have.

         You know, I'm not saying that there aren't people who like to be behind the scenes, there are.

         There are people who are quite happy to be in the same job for 40 years, have a mediocre lifestyle with six children, go on holiday for a couple of months every year. You know, go abroad and that sort of thing and do what other people may class as boring or lethargic, but actually they're comfortable and they're happy and they're enjoying themselves.

         They tend not to be professionals or personal development enthusiasts. Let's face it we're the people who sell, tell, teach, train, coach, consult, negotiate, network, educate, compete and even entertain, and we do all that because we want to *engage* in our purpose and do that in an *enterprising* way.

Now personal branding started to happen about five or six years ago. I'd never heard the term before.

It's just something that stuck, you know? It's part of the religion approach now of personal and professional development, that you have to have personal branding.

The problem with that of course, is that as soon as you say you have to have personal branding, people don't think who am I? People think what do I do? And what am I?

And then you start ... I suppose you could call it projecting. It's more important what's on the outside, the colour of this and the colour of that and let's start persuading people, because people have got this brand or that brand or the other brand and that colour.

I prefer to teach that it's about **Personal Presence**. It's about the impact that you make, it's about the impression that you leave behind.

I think if you're a professional and personal development enthusiast, you have to think about personal presence first.

You have to think about where do I fit in that room? What presence do I have in that room? Not how do I create it, but how do I find my place there? How can I be there 100%? Because if you're there 100%, your presence will attract the people in that room.

Now don't think this is about being in people's faces.

Take a party situation.

The person whose presence is quiet, having a little drink, sitting on the sofa talking to people, generally, speaking they're surrounded by people who want to listen or want to talk themselves.

The 'let's drop the trousers, put the lampshade on the head, get up on the table and have a dance person', tends to be surrounded by the people who enjoy that sort of thing.

Each one has a presence in the room, but they know what their presence should be, they know what their personal presence should be and they are more of it, because they're working to the best version of themselves.

They are gathering the following they want, and doing that because they are subconsciously skilful.

When your subconscious skills are all in line, you know what you're doing, you're happy with what you're doing, you're comfortable with what you're doing and that's where your personal presence comes from.

It comes from your **Comfortable Confidence**, which gives you your **Increased Influence** and then you will gather a group around you that enjoy your **Personal Presence**.

Envoi

You do not need to change you.

But you can change your Mind, and when you change your Mind you can change your Life and live happier ever after.

I wish you a very long and a very happy life and hope we meet in person some time or place.

Thanks for getting my work.

Meet Jonathan

Jonathan Chase has collected many accolades in his hypnotic career spanning four decades; including a Command Performance CIU Award and being lauded as "Britain's leading Hypnotist" by the Mail On Sunday.

Leaving his nursing career after five years when he started to fall over more than the patients; he's used his study of the subconscious to build international showbiz success, and to control challenges his Muscular Dystrophy brings daily.

Most of his friends had gone into the business called Show, and having been a roadie it was a natural for him to go back to twiddling knobs in lighting and sound. And hanging around with magicians, comedians, and even knife throwers, he came across his natural talent for hypnosis and suggestion.

In the hotel De France in Jersey he watched a show-band drummer hypnotise a young lady, who was then told that a toy dog a little boy was playing with, was a fully grown lion.

The resulting mayhem convinced Jonathan he had to discover more about the mind and imagination, he had to know why reality can change so quickly, and he had to find out how to get the girl out of the elevator she'd locked herself into.

That led to two years training by osmosis and reading everything he could; and understanding the subconscious took him from the Coal miners welfare and working men's clubs of his Midlands home, to headlining at the Starlight of Shaftesbury Avenue in London's West End, and all the way to the showroom stage at the Orleans Casino in Las Vegas.

Despite his worsening condition, Speaking has taken over from showbiz because it's much easier to involve his audience to personally experience his eclectic approaches from the worlds of Motivation, Mesmerism, Mentalism, Metaphysics, Hypnosis, NeuroLinguistics and Psychometrics.

Amazon Best selling Author of several popular books, Developer of the Mind STYLE psychometric profiling model, co-founder of SubSkills Training and co-host with his partner Jane Bregazzi of the When No One Else Is Looking podcast.

Jon's drive is to help second half of life, Experts, Professional Communicators and Influencers get more Profit From their endeavours, more Pleasure from their adventures and more time to enjoy Playing, achieving more success with far less stress.

Postword

Hi there, it's Jane Bregazzi

I'm incredibly lucky because as Director of BOW Books and Interviewer for this particular book, I'm allowed to be the facilitator to some awesome people's ideas, expertise and treasures being shared with the world.

Jonathan Chase who I've had the good fortune to have worked with, and lived with for nearly 20 years, is a pragmatist of the first order. Although in a wheelchair and has challenges everyday with the progression of his muscular dystrophy he still manages to be comfortable with who he is and his place in the world. He is wholly passionate about imparting his years of knowledge, to be the inspiration and motivation in people's lives.

Jonathan's talent for being the Hypnotist and Edutainer is something that is hard to replicate, but his years of observation with the subconscious mind's of others has allowed him now to create this book, solely dedicated to how you can use what you already have on-board, to find momentum in your life and business.

Unlike a foreword I'm not here to tell you to read the book; I'm here to tell you to read it again, and again, use the advice and take on the teaching.

As with all of our books, you should be able to consume this on an average commute into town, definitely while you're waiting for your cancelled flight, or over a couple of lunches.

So you can use repetition and really learn.

As with all of our authors Jonathan doesn't do fluff or fancy passages full of rhetoric, we don't do the 'bigger the book the better the content' thing.

So, go back and read this again. Make notes in the margins. Fold page corners to mark the best bits. Spill coffee and tea on the cover...

READ the book and allow it to help your life change. Enhance Your Experience and boost your business now.

(Bring your dogeared and beaten book to any event you see us advertise on our website or podcast and you may be in for a surprise!)

WNOEIL

When No One Else is Looking
PODCAST

Jonathan and Jane chat show

Subscribe on iTunes
or your favourite listening channel.

WhenNoOneElseIsLooking.com

Also by Jonathan Chase

Your Mind STYLE shapes your behaviour that is at least 50% hardwired. This is how you do the things you do. Find out why for Free at:

MindStyleApp.com
Go there Now take the test and claim your free book

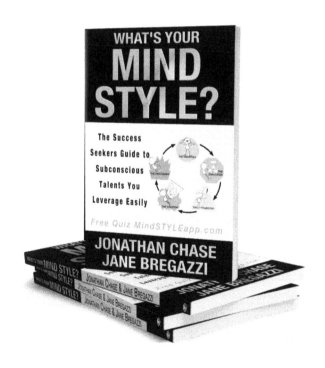

Books of Wisdom Publications
Enhancing the Experience of Life
For the most up to date information
Visit SubSkillsTraining.com

We look forward to meeting you.
Jane Bregazzi SubSkills Training

Lightning Source UK Ltd.
Milton Keynes UK
UKHW021849060219
336823UK00005B/144/P

9 781916 502635